A FIRST LOOK AT DINOSAURS

by Millicent E. Selsam
and Joyce Hunt

ILLUSTRATED BY HARRIETT SPRINGER

WALKER AND COMPANY NEW YORK

Library of Congress Cataloging in Publication Data

Selsam, Millicent Ellis, 1912-
  A first look at dinosaurs.

  Summary: Introduces the groups into which
scientists divide the more than 1000 kinds of
dinosaurs, such as lizard-hipped, bird-hipped,
plated, and armored.
  1. Dinosaurs—Juvenile literature. [1. Dinosaurs]
I. Hunt, Joyce. II. Springer, Harriett, ill.
III. Title.
QE862.D5S39 1982   567.9'1   81-71194
ISBN 0-8027-6454-1   AACR2
ISBN 0-8027-6456-8 (lib. bdg.)

28830

First published in the United States of America
in 1982 by the Walker Publishing Company, Inc.

Published simultaneously in Canada by John Wiley & Sons Canada,
Limited, Rexdale, Ontario.

ISBN: 0-8027-6454-1 Trade
ISBN: 0-8027-6456-8 Reinf.

Library of Congress Catalog Card Number: 81-71194

Printed in the United States of America

10 9 8 7 6 5 4 3 2

A *FIRST LOOK AT* SERIES

Each of the nature books for this series is planned to develop the child's powers of observation and give him or her a rudimentary grasp of scientific classification.

For Margaret Amanda Selsam

Dinosaurs lived millions of years ago.

The Age of Dinosaurs

5   195   135   65

Millions of Years Ago

Some dinosaurs were giants and others
were no bigger than turkeys.
Some had long sharp teeth and ate meat.
Others had teeth like pegs and ate plants.
Some had bumps.
Some had horns.
Some had spikes.
There were almost 1000 different kinds of dinosaurs.
How do you tell them apart?

One group of dinosaurs were meat eaters.
They walked on their hind legs and
had sharp teeth and claws.
They came in different sizes.

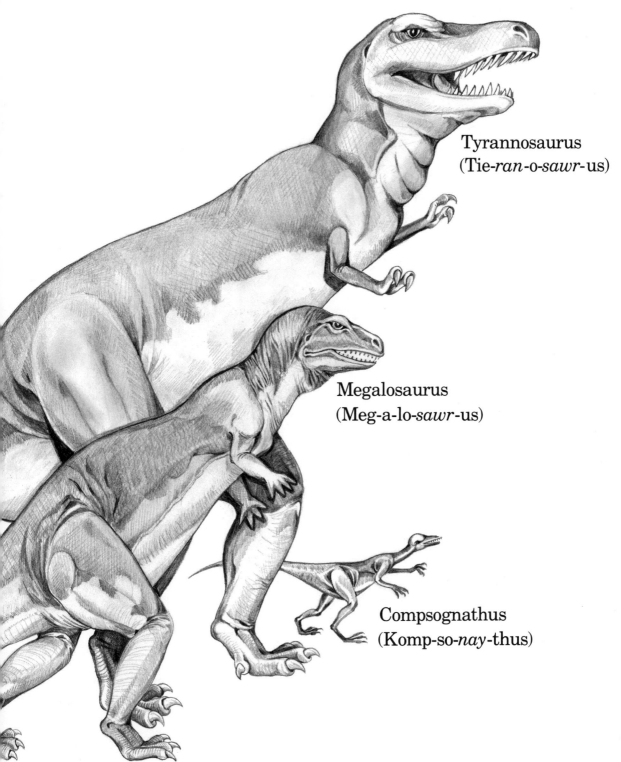

Tyrannosaurus
(Tie-*ran*-o-*sawr*-us)

Megalosaurus
(Meg-a-lo-*sawr*-us)

Compsognathus
(Komp-so-*nay*-thus)

9

Another group of dinosaurs were giant
plant eaters. They walked on all four feet.
They had very long necks and tails.
Their legs were as big as tree trunks.
Although they were all big, some were bigger than others.

Diplodocus
(Di-*plod*-oke-us)

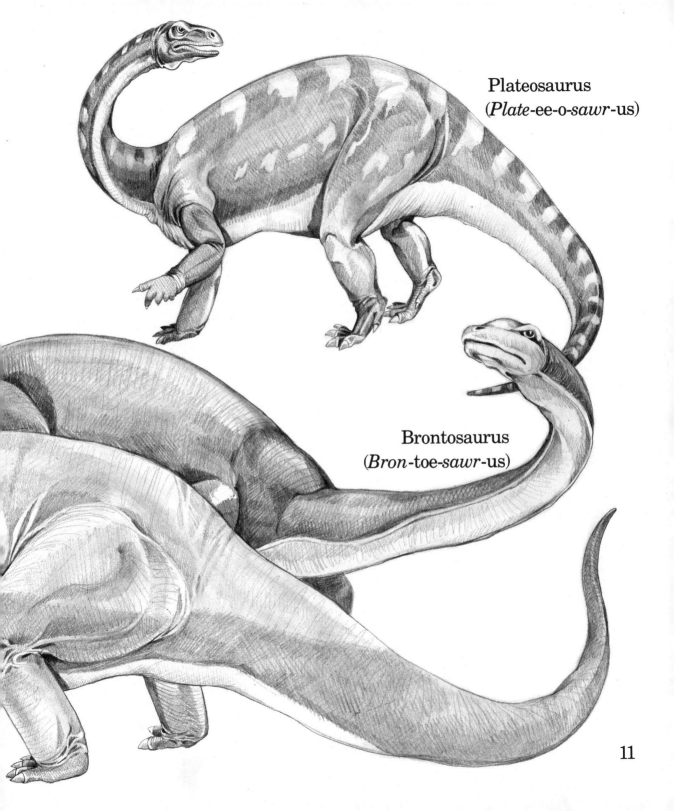

Plateosaurus
(*Plate*-ee-o-*sawr*-us)

Brontosaurus
(*Bron*-toe-*sawr*-us)

11

Even though the meat-eaters and the giant plant-eaters
looked very different, scientists found that
their hip bones were the same.
They looked like those of a lizard.
The scientists called them
lizard-hipped dinosaurs.

Here are the hip bones close up:

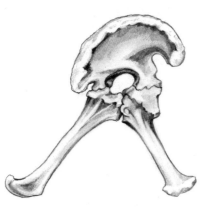

In the lizard-hipped dinosaurs,
bones 1 and 2 are wide apart,
like this:

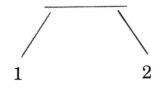

1   2

All other dinosaurs had hip bones like those of a bird.
Scientists called them *bird-hipped dinosaurs.*

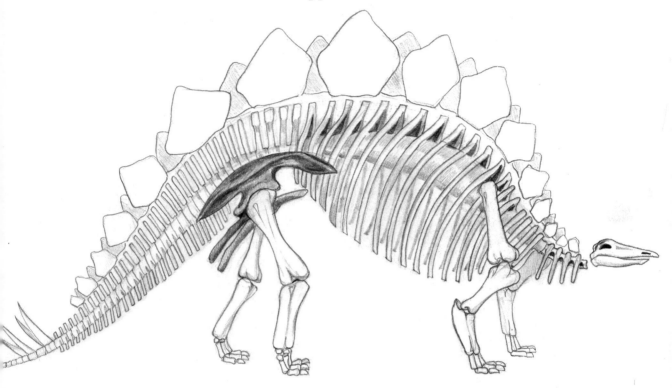

Here are these hip bones close up:

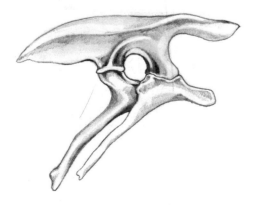

In the bird-hipped dinosaurs,
bones 1 and 2 are alongside
one another, like this:

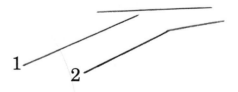

13

A Puzzle:
Here are two dinosaurs.
Can you tell which one is bird-hipped and
which one is lizard-hipped?

While there were only two kinds of lizard-hipped dinosaurs, scientists found four different kinds of bird-hipped dinosaurs. They were all plant-eaters.

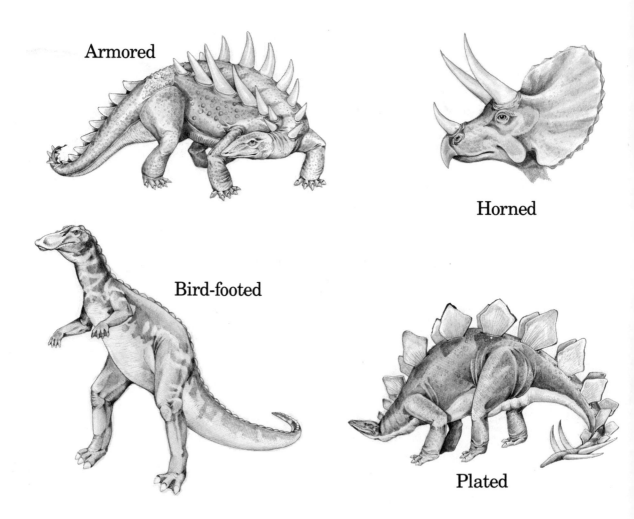

Armored

Horned

Bird-footed

Plated

The *Plated Dinosaurs* had heavy bony plates
and spikes on their backs and tails.

Which dinosaur has more plates?
Which dinosaur has more spikes?

Kentosaurus
(*Kent*-o-*sawr*-us)

Stegosaurus
(*Steg*-o-*sawr*-us)

Armored dinosaurs had spikes and plates
not only on their backs and tails but over most
of their bodies. They were low and wide and looked
like army tanks.

Find the armored dinosaur with short spikes
along its sides.
Find the one with short spikes on its back.
Find the one with long spikes on its back.

Polacanthus
(Pole-a-*kan*-thus)

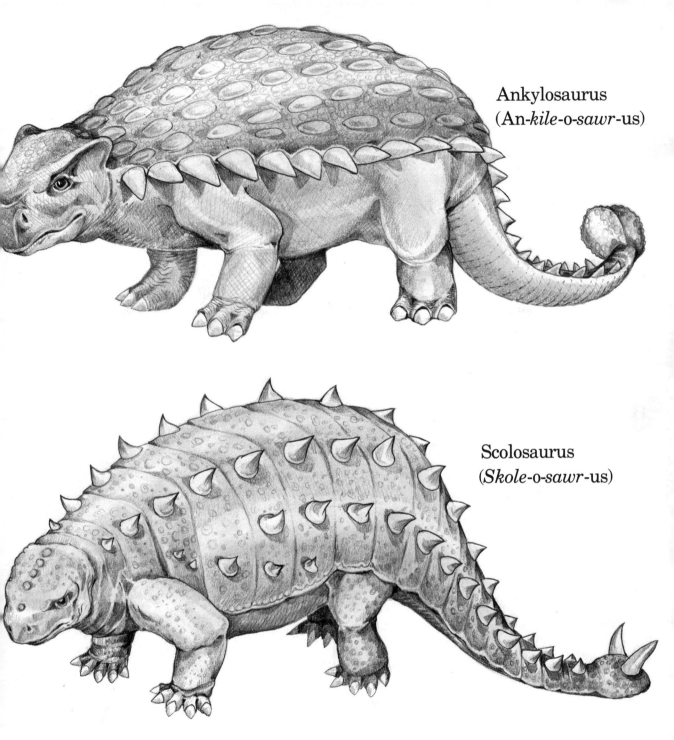

Ankylosaurus
(An-*kile*-o-*sawr*-us)

Scolosaurus
(*Skole*-o-*sawr*-us)

19

Bird-footed dinosaurs walked on
two feet like birds.
Some looked like the giant meat-eaters (p. 8-9),
but they were usually not so big and
they did not have sharp flesh-tearing teeth.
They had teeth like pegs which helped them eat plants.

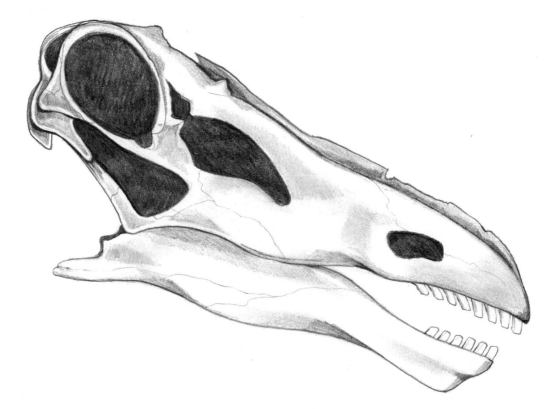

Which one has knobs and spikes on its head?

Which bird-footed dinosaur has spiky thumbs on its "hands"?

The Iguanodon (ih-*gwan*-oh-don) was one of the first dinosaurs discovered.

The Pachycephalosaurus (*pak*-ee-*sef*-a-lo-*saur*-us) is called a bonehead because its skull is very thick.

21

Some of the bird-footed dinosaurs were called *duckbills* because they had bills like ducks.

Anatosaurus
(An-*at*-o-*sawr*-us)

Many duckbills had strange crests on their heads.

Corythosaurus
(*Kor*-ith-o-*sawr*-us)

Tsintaosaurus
(Tsin-*tay*-o-*sawr*-us)

Parasaurolophus
(Par-a-sawr-*ol*-o-fus)

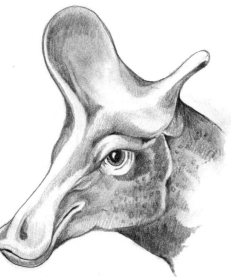

Lambeosaurus
(*Lam*-bee-o-*sawr*-us)

23

Horned dinosaurs had horns on their heads and
a thick bone collar around their necks.
They also had beaks like parrots.

Find the dinosaur with three horns.
Find the dinosaur with one horn, and spikes on
the edge of its bony collar.
Find the dinosaur with one horn.

Triceratops
(Try-*ser*-a-tops)

Monoclonius
(Mon-o-*klone*-ee-us)

Styracosaurus
(Sty-rack-o-*sawr*-us)

25

When dinosaurs lived, all the continents were joined together, and the dinosaurs could move almost all over the world.

Later the continents drifted away from each other
and oceans separated them. That is why dinosaur
bones were found in these places in the world.

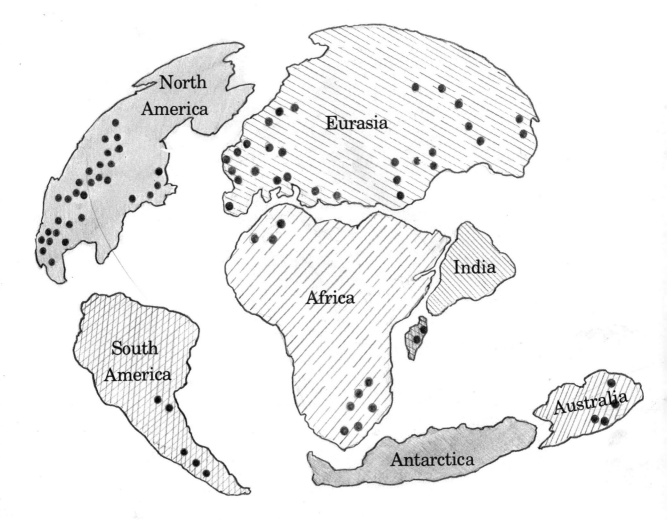

Dinosaurs died out 65 million years ago.
No one knows why. If you want to see a
dinosaur today, you have to go to a museum
to look at their bones.

New discoveries about dinosaurs are still being made.

Since 1970, fifty new kinds of dinosaurs have been found.
The biggest one yet, a giant plant-eater, was dug up in 1979.
It has no scientific name yet, but people are calling it
Ultrasaurus (ull-tra-*sawr*-us).

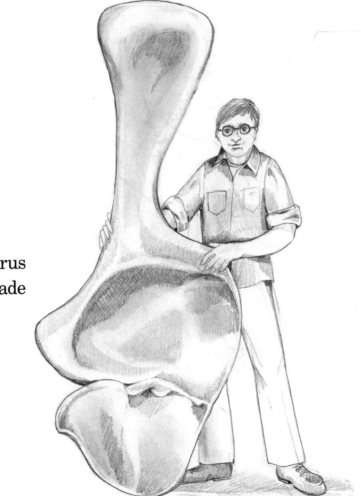

Ultrasaurus
shoulder blade

CLASSIFICATION OF DINOSAURS

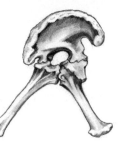

LIZARD-HIPPED DINOSAURS

1—Meat-Eaters
   Look for dinosaurs that walked on two feet
   and had sharp teeth and claws.

2—Giant Plant-Eaters
   Look for huge dinosaurs with
   long necks and tails.

BIRD-HIPPED DINOSAURS

1—Plated Dinosaurs
   Look for bony plates or spikes
   on back and tail.

2—Armored Dinosaurs
   Look for bony plates and spikes
   over most of the body.

3—Bird-footed Dinosaurs
   Look for dinosaurs that walked
   on two feet and had teeth like pegs.

4—Horned Dinosaurs
   Look for horns, beaks
   and bony collars.

31

DINOSAURS IN THIS BOOK: